# O YE JIGS AND JULEPS!

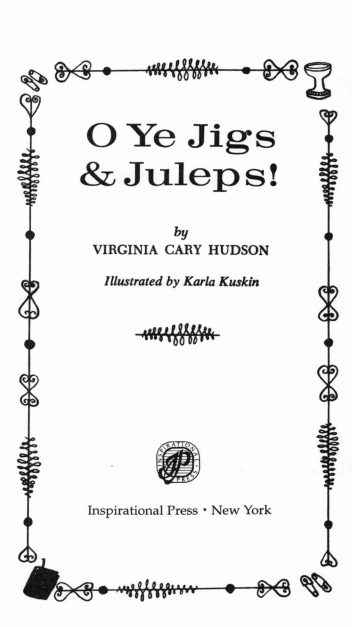

# O Ye Jigs & Juleps!

*by*
VIRGINIA CARY HUDSON

*Illustrated by Karla Kuskin*

Inspirational Press • New York

First Inspirational Press edition published in 1996.

Inspirational Press
A division of Budget Book Service, Inc.
386 Park Avenue South
New York, NY 10016

Inspirational Press is a registered trademark of Budget Book Service, Inc.

Published by arrangement with Scribner, A division of Simon and Schuster, Inc.

Library of Congress Catalog Card Number: 87-15877

ISBN: 0-88486-140-6

Printed in the United States of America.

### To Mother

"Well may her glowing heart rejoice
And tell its rapture all abroad."

P. DODDRIDGE

Although some of the incidents in this book had their bases in fact, surely the arm of coincidence is not long enough for them to have happened to any of the people named in these pages.

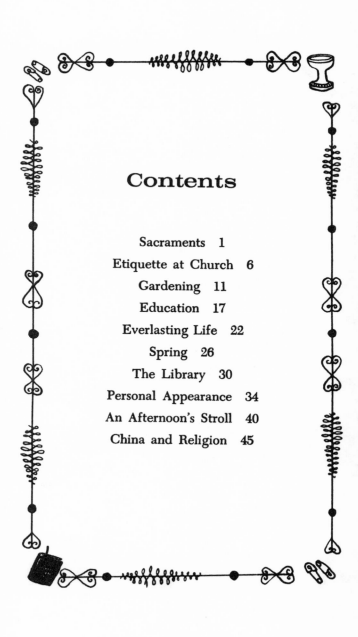

# Contents

# Sacraments

Sacraments are what you do in Church. What you do at home is something else. Cooking and sewing and running the Bissels sweeper and eating and sleeping and praying and scrubbing yourself are not sacraments.

When you are little and ugly somebody carries you in church on a pillow, and you come out a child of God and inheritor of the Kingdom of Heaven. They pour water on your head and that's a sacrament. When you are twelve you walk back in yourself with your best dress and shoes on, and your new prayer book your mother buys you, and you walk up to the Bishop, and he stands up, and you kneel down, and he mashes on your head, and you are an Episcopal. Then you are supposed to increase in spirit. Then everybody kisses you and that's a sacrament. Only I left out the bread and the wine. That's a sacrament too. I tasted some of that bread in the choir room and it tasted just like my gold fish wafers.

Then when you are married, you go back to church dressed up like you never were before in all your days. Somebody sings "Oh Promise Me" and your sweetheart is waiting up by the preacher, if he doesn't forget to come, and you get a new shiney gold band on your finger and leave town. And that's a sacrament.

Miss Molly Anderson got all ready to get married and she let me see all of her lovely clothes all spread out on the bed in the spare room. Only she didn't get married. The bridegroom forgot to come back. He traveled. And I guess he took the wrong train or something. Mrs. Anderson shut the shutters, and nobody would come to the door, and when I went around to the kitchen door to take Miss Molly some cinnamon drops, the cook says to me, she said, "Go away, scat." But Miss Molly didn't care if he did forget to come. She bought her a new bath suit with a big sailor collar, and ruffles around her knees, and she married Dr. Thomwood, and I like him. He is handsome. That old absent-minded bridegroom was always saying to me, "Little girl, isn't it time you were going home?" And I had only just got, I mean gotten there. And I barely had sat myself down in the parlor.

And then you get carried back in the Church again. But you are dead and it takes six people to lift you. And everybody cries and that's the last sacrament you are going to get. Mrs. Park was old and so sick she didn't even know her own children. Maybe she was tired fooling with them all those years and just acted like she didn't know them. When Mrs. Park died I sure didn't cry because I bet when she waked up and found she was dead she was just tickled to death.

One day we got tired of playing hop-scotch and skin the cat, so Edna Briggs said, "Let's play Baptizing." I said to Mrs. Williams, "Can we, I mean may we play Baptizing in your rain barrel?" And she said to me, she said, "Yes, indeed," and she just went on tatting. So I put on my father's hunting breeches and got Judge Williams' hat off the moose horn rack, and I dressed up like the Baptist preacher. That was when Edna ran to get all the kids. And I said to them I said, "The Lord is in his Holy Temple, keep silent and shut up." And then I said, "All you sinners come forward and hence." And nobody came but Melvin Dawson. He is just two years old. Poor little Melvin. He is so unlucky. I got him by the back of his diaper and dipped him in the rain barrel once for the Father, and once for the Son, and when it came time for the Holy Ghost, poor little Melvin's safety pin broke and he dropped in the bottom of the rain barrel, and everybody ran, and nobody would help me, and I had to turn the rain barrel over to get him out, and then I galloped him on his stomach on my pony to get the water out of him, and then I sat him inside his house, and then I went out to Mrs. Harris' house and got under her bed, and when she looked under there and saw me, all soaking wet, Mrs. Harris said, she said, "Rain and hail in Beulah land, what has happened now?" And when I told her what had happened she just patted her foot and sat, and

sat, and then she said, "You know what?" and I said, "What" and Mrs. Harris said, "The Bishop sure needs just such a barrel in the church yard to give some members I know just what little Melvin got." And then Mrs. Harris said, "Let's talk about fishing." And we did.

Thank God for fishing. Thank God for Mrs. Harris and God bless poor little Melvin. Amen.

# Etiquette
# at Church

Before I go into the house of the Lord with praise and thanksgiving, I lift up mine eyes unto the town clock from whence cometh the time to see if I am late. It is not etiquette to be late.

Do not hop, skip, jump or slide in the church vestibule. Tip. Tip all the way to your seat. Be sure and do not sit in other people's pews. Jesus wouldn't care, but other people would. Paying money makes it yours to sit in. The first thing you do is kneel down and thank the Lord for your mother and your father and your breakfast and your lunch and your dinner and your lovely wallpaper and your new pink garter belt. Then you can sit and look around just a little bit. Don't turn around and look. That is not etiquette.

Kneel when you pray, stand when you sing, and sit when you listen. On communion Sunday take off your right glove and leave it in your pew.

Don't wait until you get to the rail and the Body and the Blood comes around. Don't try to drink up all of the wine. That is not etiquette. Leave some for other people.

Never punch people in church, or giggle or cross your legs. Crossing your legs is as bad as scratching or walking in front of people or chewing gum or saying damn. Don't lose your place in the prayer book. Bow for the cross and for the Father, Son and Holy Ghost. When the choir marches back to the Vestry room and the minister calls out goodbye to the Lord until next Sunday, then you can speak to people.

The Baptist church is next door to our church. They sing as loud as they can all the time we are trying to pray. I bet the Lord can't hear one word we say. The Baptists sing about plunging sinners in a bloody fountain drawn from Emmanuel's veins. We sing about Crown Him Lord of All. I think it is much more ladylike to crown the King than to be plunging around in a bloody fountain. I took the cotton off my sore finger once and stuffed it in my ear on the Baptist side. But just once. My mother attended to that.

Of all people who come to church I love Mrs. Harris best. Mrs. Harris is Mrs. Porter's auntie and that makes her important, but Mrs. Harris doesn't care. She just goes on picking beans. She taught me to tell the young ones from the old ones, just like people. She says I am a good picker. When I ride my pony out to Mrs. Harris, she plays for me. She plays See the train go round the bend, goodbye my lover goodbye. I bet she plays that because she

7

knows I am with the railroad. Mrs. Harris is cute and when she dies I am going to cry and cry.

Mrs. Harris takes me fishing and I carry the worms and the lunch. But not in the same box. The worms are in a can. She stops the buckboard in front of my house and hollers Yoohoo. That's for me. Mrs. Harris is crippled and it is hard for her to get out. When I am with her I boost her. She says I am the best booster in town. When we get to the Meadows Creek where we fish I climb out over the shafts and let down the horse's check rein. Mrs. Harris says letting down the check rein is just like getting home and taking off your Sunday corset. But I am not a horse and I don't have a corset so I wouldn't know. When I had the measles Mrs. Harris brought me the most darling June bug with a red thread on his leg and tied him to my bed post.

Mrs. Harris lets me churn. She has a lot of cows that give milk and one that doesn't and is mean. I asked her why she kept that one and she said, "He is a necessity." All the other cows have names but that one and everything should have a name, so I got me a shingle and painted Mr. Necessity on it and nailed it on the gate where the gentleman cow stays and Mrs. Harris said she just didn't understand why she didn't think of that herself.

Etiquette is what you are doing and saying when people are looking and listening. What you are thinking is your business. Thinking is not etiquette. Hallelujah, thine the glory. Revive us again.

P.S. If you want to stay awake in church, go to bed early Saturday night. You can't go to the Altar

rail until you are 12. That is God's etiquette. You can't put on perfume until you are 16. That is Leesville etiquette. After you are confirmed your sponsors in Baptism can't be blamed for what you do. You are on your own then and if the devil gets you, it is your own fault and serves you just right.

Amen and the Lord have mercy.

# Gardening

Gardening is growing things. First you find some-body to dig up the ground, and when he tells you what he charges, you say "Too much" and get an-other somebody. After he digs and rakes, you start planting.

You start in the front with parsley, and lettuce, and onions, and radishes. Get a long string and two sticks and keep your lines straight. Then comes the beets, and the carrots, and the peas, and the bunch beans. The potatoes are over in a field by them-selves. Then comes the asparagus, and the celery, and last of all the pole beans, and the butter beans, and the sweet corn. Then you bound your garden on the north and the east with cantelopes and on the south and the west with watermelons. Then you plant sunflowers and hollyhocks in the back corners. Then you pray for the rain to come and if too much comes, you pray for it to stop. It keeps you busy all summer praying and hoeing.

Mrs. Harris and myself were picking potato bugs one day, and Mrs. Harris put down her tin can and said, "Snow and Ice in Beulah Land, here come my rich kin." And there was, I mean were, Miss Fanny Bannister and Miss Ruby Porter, all dressed up, except Miss Ruby went back home. And Miss Fanny said, "Get out of that potato patch, Sister Ada, and take off that sunbonnet and fix me a julip." And Mrs. Harris says to me, she says, "You fix it," and I did. I ran to the mint bed and got the sugar and the ice and the whiskey behind the blankets on the top shelf, and Miss Fanny said, "How much whiskey in here?" and I said, "One jigger," and Miss Fanny says, she says, "That's for faith. Where's the hope and Charity? Go back and put in two more." And I ran back to the potato patch and told Mrs. Harris what Miss Fanny said, and Mrs. Harris says, "Give her a Corinthian julip if she wants one and by the time I get in the house she won't know whether I am wearing a sunbonnet or a crown." And that's what Mrs. Harris said, and I did.

And I said, "What must I do until you come in?" and Mrs. Harris said, she said, "Play on the piano," and I said, "What must I play?" and she said, "Yankee Doodle," and I said, "Why?" and Mrs. Harris said, she said, "Since Fanny married two Yankees, that should be her favorite tune." And I played Yankee Doodle until I was about doodled out, and when Mrs. Harris came in, Miss Fanny said, "Sister Ada, are your taxes paid? Jim wants to know." And Mrs. Harris says, "Yes" but it didn't sound like yes to me. And when Miss Fanny left,

I said, "Are they paid?" and she said, "No," and I said, "How are you going to pay them?" and she said, "The cows and the chickens are going to pay it." And I said, "How about the eggs and the butter?" and she said, "The eggs are for me and the butter is for the Lord." And one day after I finished churning, I dropped the butter on the kitchen floor, and I said, "I dropped the Lord's butter," and she said, "Scrape it up, the Lord won't care, and we'll sell it just the same." And I did, and one day Mrs. Harris was sitting on the milk stool patting her foot, and she said, "How would you like a garden party?" and I said, "One of those stiff ones like Miss Fanny gave my mother?" And Mrs. Harris said, "Heaven forbid, I mean a real party." And she did.

I made a list of all my friends, then I was ashamed because it might be too long. The children at the Leesville Orphanage took up one whole page. And my P.S. I had was the little colored boys down on the station platform. Because they are black and raggedy I put them P.S. But Mrs. Harris said to tell them to bring their banjo and mouth harp, and they did. And Mrs. Harris said, "And now the most important friend you have for the guest of honor," and I said, "The Bishop, only he wouldn't come," and Mrs. Harris said, "What do you mean he wouldn't come, with the church roof leaking and Ruby Porter in town?" And he did and so did everybody.

And when they all got there, I whispered to Mrs. Harris, "Now is a good time to get all the weeds out of the flower borders." And she said, "How?"

and I said, "Watch." And I said, "Everybody line up, advance and pull." And I showed them where the weeds were and everybody started pulling. The Bishop too, except he was the slowest puller we had. When I got around to see how he was doing, he wasn't doing so good. So I got him a chair to sit on, and I asked Mrs. Harris if she thought he would like a Corinthian julep, and she said, "Just the thing, fix it" and I did, and I said, "Drink it," and he did, and after that he felt well enough to play London Bridge, Leap Frog and Skip-to-my-Lou.

And then we brought the little box organ out under the tree, and while Mrs. Harris was playing Dixie and all her jigs, it was time for the little colored boys to dance. And they were scared, and I pushed them out on the grass, and I said, "Dance" and they said, "If you will," and I did. I put one on each side and we danced Spread the Eagle, Buck and Wing, Go Down Moses and Kitten-on-the Keys. Then the orphans danced the Virginia Reel and then I decided I was going to make Mrs. Harris and the Bishop dance. And I did. I told them I would play Come All Ye Faithful in rag time or waltz time, and the Bishop said he thought waltz time would be best. My mother told me if I didn't quit coming home from church and playing the hymns in rag time she didn't know what on earth she would do. So now I rag them up on Mrs. Harris' piano.

And Mrs. Bannister sent the ice cream all the way from the Women's Exchange in Middleton, only I don't know why they call it a, I mean an, exchange, because while I was waiting for Sue Stevens to get her teeth straightened I took my sling shot in the exchange to trade it for a bag of cookies, and it wasn't any exchange at all, and I wanted to know why they didn't mean what they said, and they asked me to please do them just one favor, and I said, "What?" and they said to please go away, and I did, only I never will believe any signs I read any more. And Miss Susie Grenfell baked the cakes for the party and the orphans ate so much they had to untie their sashes.

I never will forget that wonderful party the longest day I live, and when I went home I rode backwards on my pony Betty Talbot's father gave me, so I could wave to Mrs. Harris as far as I could see. And if Mrs. Harris and myself are lucky enough to be in Heaven at the same time, I know what we can do when things get dull. We can give a garden party. I sure hope God didn't forget to plant a garden in Heaven.

O ye Sun and Moon, oh ye beans and roses, oh ye jigs and juleps, Bless ye the Lord, Praise Him and Magnify Him Forever. Amen.

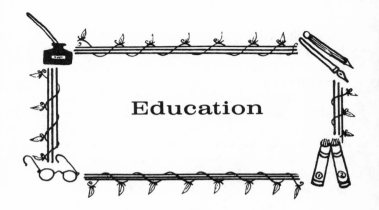

# Education

Education is what you learn in books, and nobody knows you know it but your teacher. I asked Mrs. Harris when we were plaiting rags for her kitchen rug what good Marco Polo would ever do me, and Mrs. Harris said education gave you satisfaction, but I had rather be ignorant and have fun than be educated and have satisfaction.

We had a tea up at our school when we hung Mrs. Porter's portrait in the hall, and the Bishop came and so did all the ministers from all the towns, and they sure were a doleful lot. I guess thinking about all the heathens made them sad. Our Principal said for me to show them over the school and I did. I showed them everything there was to see, including the big girls' pickled frog and dissected cat. Mrs. Megan, the housekeeper, was just furious when I took them to the kitchen, but I thought the new Detroit Jewel stove and the big white mountain ice cream freezer were well worth seeing.

And when they passed around the tea I knew the Bishop would want more sugar. He always does. So I put two lumps in my pinafore pocket and dropped them in his cup so he wouldn't get his fingers sticky and Miss Blazer sure glared at me. And the Bishop talked about Mrs. Porter being a great educator and that gave me an idea. I was tired of that tea anyway, and with Miss Blazer glaring at me I got more tired than ever, and I decided that if Mrs. Porter was a great educator, she would be the very one to help me with my arithmetic before the big test, so I went up on Tulip Hill to her house, after I got my book.

And when the butler came to the door and I asked if I might please see Miss Ruby, he stuck his stomach out at me and raised his chin way up high and he said, "Mistress Porter was in New York," and I thought if Miss Ruby was a great educator her mother should be one too, and I asked if I might please see Miss Fanny, and he puffed himself all up again and he said to me, he said, "Mistress Fanny will receive you in the gold room." And while I was waiting to be received, I sat in all the little gold chairs and stood on a gold stool and looked at myself in a gold mirror and pretended like I was a princess, and I looked at the she wolf on a gold table with poor little Romulus and Remus sitting down beside her as naked as jaybirds, only jaybirds aren't naked, they have feathers.

And when Miss Fanny finally did come in, I thought she never would, she said to me, she said, "Where is sister Ada?" Just because Mrs. Harris takes me everywhere she goes, I guess people think

18

I take Mrs. Harris everywhere I go, but I don't. I am busy, and if Mrs. Harris followed me on my trips, she never would get her churning done. And I told Miss Fanny what the Bishop said, and I asked her if she would help me with my arithmetic, and she did.

Miss Fanny is sweet and so pretty, only she wasn't much help. She just kept chewing on her pencil, and after she took off her jeweled dog collar and her shoes, she said, "Maxwell, come here." That's the butler. And he came, and she said, "Stand over there," and he stood, and she said, "Maxwell, how much education have you had?" and he said, "One year at Oxford, Madam" and she said, "Why didn't you finish?" and he said, "The family funds ran out, Madam," and she said, "I know exactly what you mean, don't say any more, but tell me how much are nine times seven." And he said, "Sixty-three, Madam." And she said, "Come here, Maxwell, and sit down," and he said, "Really, Madam" and he sat beside her and she said, "Have some crumpets, Virginia, and maybe a taste of wine."

And the wine was in the most beautiful frosted bottle with purple grapes hanging down the sides, and when I poured the wine in the glass, it ran down in the stem and looked so cute. And I drank it all and the crumpets were good, but the wine was better, and by the time I poured me out four or five glasses so I could watch it run down in the stem, Miss Fanny and Maxwell sounded so far away, and the chair seemed so soft and I leaned back and thought about poor little Romulus and

20

Remus having to build Rome on seven hills without any help, and then I heard Miss Fanny say, "The child is almost asleep, it is time for her nap, drive her home." And he did.

And I said to Edith, she's our cook, "Send for the Doctor," and she did, and Doctor said he would come, and he did. And Edith said, "Get in bed," and I did, and when Dr. Reddings came I was so glad to see him, I just love Dr. Reddings, and I said, "Cross your heart and hope to die if you ever tell," and he crossed his heart and hoped to die, and I said, "I am drunk." And he said, "Edith get a pan," and she did. And he said, "Drink this," and I did. And then he sat in a chair, and up came the sandwiches and the tea and the crumpets and the wine.

And when my mother got home from Middleton on the trolley car, she said plenty. And when I thought she had said everything there was to say, she still had plenty left. And the next day after school she said, "Put away those roller skates and sit down," and she reached in the book shelves and blew the dust off of her Women's Christian Temperance Union book and she said, "Read it every word" and there was a big picture of a green snake wrapped around a wine glass with his tongue sticking out, and I read all about whiskey making people have wild fits so they have to be locked up, and I didn't see why I should have to read all afternoon about whiskey when all I drank was a little wine.

And now Hallelujah and God forbid. Amen.

# Everlasting Life

Most of the things you get somebody dies so you can get it, but you have to die your own self to get Everlasting Life.

When you are as dead as a doornail, God gives it to you, and you can't get rid of it. You can't buy it, or sell it, or trade it. You have to keep it whether it suits you or not. When you take it to Heaven with you, that's good, but when you have to take it along with you to Hell, that's different. Bishop Jordan told me Everlasting Life was God's precious gift, and I told him if it was just the same with God, I could think of things I would like better.

If I ever get to Heaven, I will see my mother and my father and my grandmother and my grandfather and all of my cousins. That is, maybe, all of them. I bet Mrs. Harris will be there. I hope God lets us go fishing. When you go to heaven with your Everlasting Life that makes you an angel, and Peter, or Moses, or somebody, lines you all up and passes out the crown and the harps. I

**sure** am glad I take music lessons. Mrs. Harris and myself can play a duet, like we do on her piano. We play jigs. I take the chords and she takes the tune. Then she plays the whole thing, and I take up old Nellie and dance.

Nellie was Mrs. Harris' beautiful cow, and when she took the colic and died, Mrs. Harris had her skinned, and put her on the floor. That skinning turned old Nellie from a cow into a rug. Two little colored boys taught me to do that kind of dancing, down on the station platform, waiting for my father's train to come in. They taught me the Buck

and Wing and Spreading the Eagle. I hope my little brothers have grown since they have been in Heaven. If they can't walk yet, I bet carrying them around Heaven will sure make my back tired.

Everybody grows wings in Heaven, and then I can fly, and that will be wonderful. I haven't decided yet just where I will go. Miss Ruby Porter says "Paris is beautiful in the Spring." Maybe I will go there. I sure hope I don't get already for the trip, and then start molting like my canary bird. I sure will need all of my feathers to get across the ocean and back again to Heaven.

I sure am glad that Jesus is going to be in Heaven because if I get in trouble he will be there to help me out. When my mother sews on her new Wilcox and Gibbs, she sings "What a friend we have in Jesus." I sure hope she knows what she is singing about. Heaven sure is far away, and hard to get to. You don't hear much talking about Heaven. You just hope you get there. I sure am doing my very best. I sure hope I make it.

But you sure hear plenty about Hell at the Baptist Church. When I go with Darthea, that preacher hollers himself red in the face about Hell. When you get to hell with your Everlasting Life, the devil waves his pitchfork and turns it into Everlasting Damnation, and he builds a fire under you, and you wail and gnash your teeth. If poor Mrs. Columbia Stonington ever goes to hell, the devil sure will be surprised when it comes her time to stand up and gnash her teeth, because her dentist pulled her teeth out. He just kept on pulling until they were all gone. There sure is going to be a lot going on in Hell. Nero, and Herod, and Judas, and Jezabel will all be there. You sure will meet a lot of interesting people. I sure hope I don't get a horn stuck in me in the mix up.

I have one horn hole in my leg already. But I didn't get it in Hell. I got it in Arkansas. I was wearing my red sweater, and I didn't get both of my legs over the fence in time. Just one of them. That's why I have a horn hole in the other one. When I got back I made the kids pay me 5 cents to see my Arkansas horn hole, and I got my mission box full. But I let the Bishop see it free. He was sitting in our parlor waiting for my mother to come downstairs when I told him about my mission box, and I rattled it for him, and he said he never had seen a, I mean an, Arkansas horn hole in all his days and he thought it was well worth 25 cents. So I pulled down my stocking, he looked good, and gave me a quarter.

There is not a thing you can do about your Everlasting Life. You are going to get it, and you have to keep it. God sure was good to make Heaven for us, as long as we can't stay dead, but have to go somewhere, but why he doesn't do something about the devil, and close up Hell, I don't know. If I have to go to Hell, I sure hope I go to the one for Episckpalians, and don't, by mistake, get pushed in that horn punching, and tail wagging, red hot blazing one the Baptists are going to have.

The Lord have mercy. Christ have mercy. Lord have mercy. God bless the Bishop. God bless my mission box, and Jesus be my friend and help me if you can, please. Amen, and Be It So.

# Spring

Spring is beautiful, and smells sweet. Spring is when you shake the curtains, and pound on the rugs, and take off your long underwear, and wash in all the corners. Spring is when the carpet tacks come up, and all the blinds come down. In the Spring horses and mules have colts, and Tillie Unger has a baby. The doctor says "goodbye until next year." The priest says "how very sweet." And my grandmother says "how perfectly horrible."

The best thing about Spring is Easter and your new hat. Mine comes from Best & Co. My hat always has a ribbon. I will be glad when I am 14 and can have a flower. One time my ribbon is white. One time it is blue. I like red, but my mother says no. Mrs. Daniels has a beautiful pink rose on her hat. She sprays rose perfume on her rose, and after church she lets me smell it. I bet if she walked home instead of riding, a big bee would follow her all the way.

I like bees. I hunt for them and slap them down with my base ball mitt. Then I mash them and put them in a bottle. When I have ten, Nelson Brady has to give me his best agate.

Spring is when you draw a circle in the dirt with your finger, if you don't have a stick, and win all of the boys' marbles. My mother rubs lemon on her hands to make them white. I rub salt on my shooting thumb to make it tough. Spring is when

you put ladders up high and scrape out gutters, and when you put ladders down low and clean out cisterns.

I had a very good idea that Mr. Hamilton was going to find a tom cat in his cistern. Oscar Sargent bet me my whole bag of gum drops that Miss Nelly McDonnell's cat couldn't scratch himself out if we buried him. I bet he could. But if he could, he didn't. Oscar says to me, he says, "What do people do with dead bodies?" And I said to Oscar, "they tie rocks on them and throw them in the river." And Oscar says, "but we don't have a river." And I said, "Mr. Hamilton has the biggest, deepest cistern in town." And now if Oscar says I told him to put Miss Nelly's tom cat in Mr. Hamilton's cistern, he is just adding up 2 and 2 and getting five. Miss Nelly bought a can of salmon and called Kitty, Kitty the whole long day.

Spring is when the sap comes up and the flowers start blooming and the young men start up their courting. If they are poor, they walk you up one side of the street and down the other. But if they have money, and are not stingy, they come for you in a high buggy and put a linen duster on your lap.

I can't find out one thing from people except about geography, and arithmetic, and etiquette, and religion. I can't find out a thing about courting. I sure will feel silly if anybody ever comes courting me. I asked my mother what I should talk about while I was courting. She said not to worry, she felt sure I would not be "lacking in conversation" whatever that means. When I have my children, if I ever learn anything about courting, I am going to tell them what they ask me. I am going to answer all my children's questions and not start up that sniffing, and rolling my eyes like my mother does.

In the Spring, the church gets cleaned, and Jesus face gets washed on the big altar window. I don't like that picture. Jesus standing there knocking on that door every Sunday with nobody to open it. And when it storms and the rain comes and runs down the back of his neck, I feel sad. I cheer myself up by thinking about picnics, and clover chains, and birthday cakes. When I grow big, and get me a lot of green folding money, I am going to get the Bishop to let me chop that sad old window up. I will give a chopping party in the church yard and serve lemonade and pound cake. And then I will buy a happy window like none of those pew-sitters ever saw before in all their days. I am going to buy them the most beautiful and stylish guardian angel God ever had in Heaven, with big fluffy wings spread out over all the whole world.

Spring is back and next Sunday Jesus rises again from the dead, only He never was dead. How could he preach in hell and be going around in Paradise if he was, I mean were, dead? Jesus being dead is just a saying anyway, like "a stitch in time" or "the last one to the hitching post is a cry baby." But if they want to raise him from the dead over and over every year it is all right with me. Now Spring is back again and next Sunday the choir is going to raise him up.

Hallelujah, Hallelujah, Hallelujah. Glory three times also, and Amen twice.

# The Library

The Library is full of dust. Mrs. Simons sits in the middle and George Washington hangs in the hall. In the library are three kinds of books. Books people like to read. Books people do not like to read, and books people never will read. Mrs. Simons says people like books with spice. Spice comes from India. The porter mops at the Library. He is black and so is his mop water. Mrs. Simons is white and George Washington is dead. The porter says, "Move along." Mrs. Simons says, "Where is your card, you owe me three cents." George Washington says, "In time of peace prepare for war." The library has a wide stair rail. That is where I split my best bloomers. My mother said, "Have you been in Dr. Grenfell's tree?" "No." "Have you been on Mrs. Bannister's gate post?" "No." "Then where have you been?" "Only sliding down the Library stair rail to get a better view of Washington."

The library is where my father took his check book when I broke the window. I was only trying to kill a fly. It would take too long to tell you what my mother said. My father said the window was old and thin. So is Mrs. Simons. I bet if I killed a fly on her she would crack too.

In the library are signs. Silence. Mrs. Simons must not know they are there. She talks the whole long day. The library is never busy but Mrs. Simons is. She hurries home and brings supper in a sack. I bet she is glad she hasn't any husband. Then she would have to cook. Mrs. Simons has two children, Gordon and Katherine. He plays the organ and she whistles. But not in the same place at the same time. The playing goes on at church and the whistling goes on in the kitchen. The reason I know so much about Mrs. Simons is because she lives next door. One time she thought I broke the picket off the fence. But I didn't. It came off its own self when I squeezed through to smell her poppies. And after all that trouble they didn't even smell.

Miss Lulu Johnson comes to the library looking for her ancestor. I wonder who she thinks she is fooling. Miss Lulu knows ancestors are on walls and in coffins. I bet if she ever finds him in that book he will be mashed flatter than my cabbage rose.

On one side of the library is the Carter Planters Bank. Mrs. Carter came to our house. She had a cramp in her leg. She called it Charliehorse. After that she had a baby. Mrs. Carter named him Charlie. I bet she named him for the horse. Mrs. Carter is very old and she wanted to surprise Mr.

31

Carter about the baby. She went to Rome and
stayed and stayed and stayed. I bet she stayed over
a year. When Mr. Carter got the telegram about
Charlie being born, Mr. Carter fell out of the chair
and butt his head on the bank floor. My father
picked him up and my father hurt his back because
Mr. Carter is too fat. I hope I never get fat.

On the other side of the library is Dr. Lothrop's stable. Dr. Lothrop sits outside and the horses stand up inside. Dr. Lothrop is fat too. He has a big gold watch chain stretched all the way across his stomach. It looks kind of greenish to me. I mean Dr. Lothrop's watch chain, not his stomach. Dr. Lothrop is Miss Sarah Foley's beau. They walk in the graveyard and rock on her porch. Dr. Lothrop said to Miss Sarah, "Miss Sarah will you please ma'am marry me." Her brother said, "No." Now she walks and rocks by herself. My father keeps his saddle horse at Dr. Lothrop's stable until he builds one, along with a house, a chicken coop, a dog pen and a flower box. My father said to Dr. Lothrop he said, "Dr. Lothrop, Miss Sarah looks badly she is so thin," and Dr. Lothrop was combing our horse's tail, and all he said was, "The nearer the bone, the sweeter the meat."

The library is a memorial. A memorial is something that somebody says or gives or builds after you are dead and can't hear it or get it or see it.

And now may God grant us all a good night's rest and not let the fire whistle blow. Amen. Hallelujah and so be it as it may.

# Personal Appearance

Personal appearance is looking the best you can for the money. When I dress up I never can slip out the door. My mother says, "Come here" and I do, and she says, "Now turn around," and I do. But before you dress up, you have to scrub yourself clean all over. My mother says I don't spend enough time in my bath, so I hung my clock on the hot water bottle hook in the bathroom, and when I was through I got me a piece of paper and a pencil, and I wrote down "Face five minutes, ears five minutes, one arm five minutes, two arms, ten minutes, one leg five minutes, two legs ten minutes, back five minutes." Then I stopped writing. And when I got dressed, I went back and wrote, "P.S. I forgot my stomach."

I like Davenport scrubbing better. When I visit my grandmother, everybody washes in a pan in the kitchen, after you lock the door and pull down both shades. Then you start at the top and go down, and then you can't miss anything. I get tired of that same old thing. Sometimes I start at the bottom and wash up.

When somebody loves you, personal appearance don't, I mean doesn't count. Mrs. Harris looks just as pretty to me in her sunbonnet squatting in the turnip bed as she does sitting in church in her ostrich trimmed horse hair braided hat. Of course, when you finish with your personal appearance, if you are born pretty, that helps also. When Mr. Henry Watterman went to the Holt House to the ball, when the ball was over, he wrote in his newspaper that my mother was the prettiest woman in Carolina, only she wasn't married, much less my mother then, and when she was my mother, and saw me, I bet she thought she was stung, because I think I look horrible.

And when we moved to Leesville, everybody wanted to know what she looked like, and they started coming, and one day when she was tired and started crying because the cook didn't come, she said, "I wish these women would stay at home until I get my good dishes unpacked." And I thought I would help her, and I put a sign on the screen and it said, "please stay at home until I unpack my good dishes." And I found out I didn't help a bit. She had one of her fits, and I whispered to my father, "What's the matter with her?" and he whispered back, "She's having an Irish fit," and I whispered to my father, "Why?" and he whispered back, "Because she's Irish" and I whispered to my father, "Why don't you ever have one?" and he whispered back, "Because I'm English." And my

father sure is English. The kids on my street can't understand one word he says.

When you put on your personal appearance, you have to fasten every single button on your high top shoes, and get your hair ribbon loops just exactly even. When I was sitting on the fence at the Leesville orphanage waiting for the orphans to come, poor little Louise told me she never had a hair ribbon in all her days, and I went to Mr. Rosenberg's store. He is Eleanora's father, and when I go to his house, he gives me a big piece of pie for rocking Gerald to sleep. Gerald just loves hymns. And I said to Mr. Rosenberg, "Can I owe you for this pink hair ribbon to take to an orphan who never had one in all her days?" and he said, "Yes" and it was twenty-five cents, and I took it and tied it on her. And Louise's hair is gold like my mother's.

I bet Mr. Henry Watterman sure would think it looked pretty if he could see it, and when I was worried to death where I was going to get twenty-five cents, here came that Tim Summerfield, acting smart with a new fifty cents for his birthday to buy paint for his bicycle. He is one of those Presbyterians and I thought of something. I said, "I bet you twenty-five cents the Presbyterians believe in procrastination" and he said they didn't and I took him up to Dr. Briggs' house. He is their preacher. And I told him what I wanted to know. And he said the Presbyterians sure did believe in procrastination and the pledge cards proved it. And I asked him if he had change for fifty cents and he said yes, and I got my twenty-five cents and took

37

it to Mr. Rosenberg, and Tim ran home crying and his mother called my father's office and said if he wasn't careful he would have a gambler on his hands, and he said it looked like he already had one, and she said gambling was terrible, and he said it certainly was when you lost, and he gave me twenty-five cents to take to Tim with a can of paint for his birthday, and he didn't even thank me.

He even set his mother's Morris chair on fire practising smoke screen signals, and he said I made him sick, and so did my father, with his funny put-on talk, and I said my father couldn't help it because his A was broad, and he said my father was knocking all the dishes in town off the shelves blasting his dynamite, and I said Mr. Wilton Smoot told him to knock them off, and he said Mr. Wilton Smoot and my father were both just dirty old railroaders. And that's when it happened. He was opening his paint to see what color it was, and I grabbed it and sat on him and poured it all on his head, and his mother called up my father again, and my father said he didn't know anything else to do but let me give Tim a can of paint remover for Christmas.

The older you get the worse your personal appearance gets. More aggravating every year. When you get as big as you are going to get you have to manicure your nails. I sure will hate that. Then you have to put stays behind your ears in your shirt waist collar, and for the Lord's sake, put plenty of extra hooks and eyes on your placket so your corset string won't hang out. My grandmother has her dressmaker put her placket on the side. She says

**when** she stands up in church she is not taking any chances.

The Lord please help us with our personal appearance. Glory Hallelujah, and Revive us Again. Amen.

# An Afternoon's Stroll

When I go strolling down to the post office to buy stamps to write to my cousins, my mother says, "Don't walk on the Court House side." That is where the checker players sit. When I get to the pansy bed, my mother calls, "Don't walk past the barber shop." That is where the men take off their collars. When I get to the linden trees, my mother says, "Don't pass the saloon." That is where the door is sawed off at the top and the bottom and the music box is. So I walk in the middle of the street and jump the stepping stones.

And when I get back, my mother says, "Oh, Oh, your best ankle strap slippers, they are covered with dust." Some people sure are hard to please. If the Court House is on one side of the street, and the barber shop and saloon are on the other side of the street, and I can't walk in the middle, I guess my mother wants me to fly to the places I go just like St. Francis of Assisi. That's what the Catholics say.

40

But the priest drinks all the wine at that church and maybe he was just seeing things.

Strolling is walking slow and easy like getting married. I guess walking slow getting married is because it gives you time to maybe change your mind. You stroll when you are a baby sitting in your carriage. You stroll when you are a young lady and have a beau. Then you stroll when you are an old lady and it doesn't matter where you are going or when you get back. When you stroll you get dressed up. Only when I stroll up on Holton Street, I wear my fighting clothes.

Holton Street is where I have my worse trouble. That is another part of town. That is where the Campbellites live. They asked me to their old church party and my mother made me go. And I wore my hat and it was summer, and Alice Coleman laughed because I had on my hat. I said to her, I said, "You shouldn't go in church without your hat." And she said, "You should too." and I said, "You shouldn't," and she said, "You should," and I said, "you shouldn't," then she said, "Who said so?" and I said, "St. Paul said so," and she said, "He didn't" and I said, "He did," and she said, "He didn't" and I said, "He did," and she said, "Fooie on St. Paul," and that is when I slapped her. Once for St. Paul, and I slapped her for the whole state of Christ's church universal and then I pinched her for myself. That slapping was righteous indignation, but that pinch was my own and the devil's idea.

She ran home from the church party screaming and yelling, but I stayed and ate my ice cream.

And Miss Billie called my mother up. Miss Billie is Alice's mother. Whoever heard of a mother named Billie? My mother made me sit in my chair one whole hour and read St. Paul. She said that was a good day to read *all* St. Paul said. So I read about enduring all things and not to behave yourself unseemly. But I bet one thing. I bet St. Paul didn't know any Campbellites and didn't ever go strolling up on Holton Street.

I asked Mrs. Scofield if she would please give me a Persian kitten when her cat had one, and she said there weren't going to be any kittens, and I said, "Why?" and she said just because her cat's name was Henry. And if Mrs. Scofield's cat can't have kittens because it is named Henry, how can Alice's mother have her when her name is Billie?

Mrs. McLean strolls in her flower garden with a shawl around her shoulders and her chain and fan around her neck. Strolling time is before four and five and that makes it just right for me, because then I am dressed up. I sit up on the fence and wait for Mrs. McLean to ask me over. My mother won't let me go unless I am invited. Then we stroll all around the little paths and Mrs. McLean tells me the name of everything. She must sit up all night learning those names. I am glad my mother didn't name me Spirea Van Houtti. I asked Mrs. McLean is that catalogue talk Spanish, and she said it was Botany. I asked her where they talked Botany and she said all over the world. I asked her if Botany was dead and she said no and I told her Latin was dead, and when I asked her how long she thought Botany would live, she changed the subject. She is good at that.

I love Mrs. McLean. She is my good sweet neighbor, but I have thought for some time she was a little cracked. When we sit on her garden bench, I get to hurting. Those iron grapes sure are hard. Mrs. McLean is fatter in the back than I am and I guess that is why she can sit there so long. Judge Williams has a bench. That's what Mrs. Williams says. She says the judge is on the bench today. And

I went down to the court house to see for myself if his bench was as hard as Mrs. McLean's bench. If it was, I was going to give him a pillow for Christmas.

And after I went all the way down to the court house, there Judge Williams was sitting in a big soft chair. He sits up there and says, "thirty days and thirty dollars." Our house boy is named Robert and he looks mighty polite and harmless tipping around our table passing the Sally Lunn, but on Saturday nights he gets his razor out and he prowls and slashes around. That's how I know Judge Williams says thirty days and thirty dollars. Robert is lazy too. When my father is out of town blasting off dynamite, Robert says to me, he says, "I'll give you a nickel to curry Mack." Mack is our carriage horse. And I say, "sure," and I get up on Mack's back and brush as far as I can reach, then I get under his feet and finish brushing. I always get the nickel first and then I put it in my mission box. I get the nickel for the missionaries first because I don't trust people that, I mean who, carry razors.

When you stroll you never hurry back, because if you had anything to do, you wouldn't be strolling in the first place. If I get a zero on this, for fighting in church, I just don't care. That Alice Coleman, insulting the saints in glory. Maybe next time I will get 99. I never get 100. Something is always wrong. Maybe one day I will. Maybe one day the Lord will help me get 100.

Praise God from whom all blessings flow. Selah. Oh lamb of God that taketh away the sins of the world, grant me peace and not zero. Amen.

# China and Religion

China is far away across the ocean. I go to the ocean every summer to meet my cousins. One I love very much. I am praying to the Good Lord to make me love the other just a little.

China is very big. It is way up North and way over East and way down South and way out West. Way out West there is a big wall 1400 miles long and 20 feet high and 8 feet thick. On top of it is a smooth road. If I ever go to China, I hope I do not forget my roller skates. China has millions of people. The tall ones live up North and the short ones live down South. My grandmother says my legs are too long. I would have to live up North and that would be awful. But maybe China does not have Yankees. In China everybody eats rice. The poor ones do not have turkey and gravy and cranberries. Silk comes from China so they grow silk worms to make the silk. I do not like worms. When there is a caterpillar on the front door I go in the back door.

China is high. Mountains. China is low. Valleys. China has long rivers. People live on boats. They do not have to pay taxes or cut grass. If they do not like their neighbors, they can move without packing things up. Missionaries go to China. Missionaries are people who are Christians who try to make other people Christians too. They can't get people to come to church here and listen so they go to China to see if the Chinese will come and listen. I bet they can't even talk like a Chinaman. A long trip for nothing if you ask me.

In China there are two classes of people, the upper crust and the under crust, just like there is in Leesville. China has three religions stated by Mr. Confuscius, Mr. Tao and Mr. Buddha. Leesville is ahead of China. Leesville has seven religions, Catholics, Episcopalians, Methodists, Baptists, Campbellites, Presbyterians, and Holly Rollers. I sure would love to see them roll, but my mother won't let me go. The Chinese temples are very big and all paid for. They are two thousand years old. Maybe in two thousand years we will have our church paid for. They may have my four dollars if they want it.

Mr. Lincoln said my grandfather's money was no good and he had to burn it all up. Now Mr. Wilton Smoot sends us money every month. He never forgets but he never sends enough. My mother calls it a salary. I sure hope we fight that Civil War over some day. Fighting is bad. It makes you mad and gets you all mussed up. I never fight unless some brat slaps me first. Then I fold up my good hair ribbon and finish what they start.

Mr. Confuscius told the Chinese they must not do to anybody what they did not want that other body to do to them. He told them never to lie or steal, but to think beautiful thoughts and to obey your parents and your grandparents, and all others in authority. He told them they could keep their ancestors in boxes and sit them at the table on feast days. I would love to keep my grandmother and stuff her and sit her in a chair on Christmas.

When Mr. Confuscius finished telling the people to be good and kind, Mr. Tao started up on them. He said Mr. Confuscius was just right, all but one thing. Mr. Tao said they would live again and they must share with others and pray and not eat so much and seek Salvation.

When Mr. Tao was worn out, Mr. Buddha started up. It must be exciting to be a Prince. He left his wife (I bet she ragged him) and went off to preach and never did come back. Mr. Buddha told them that Mr. Confuscius and Mr. Tao were just right about all but one thing. What good was Salvation if you couldn't use it. Just like a nickel and no candy. So he told them about heaven, only he called it Navirna. His seven paths for getting there were seven rules for living. They are just like our Commandments, only different words. Mr. Confuscius and Mr. Tao and Mr. Buddha couldn't tell the Chinese about Jesus because he had not been born. It sure is a pity Jesus didn't take a trip to China to do his own talking instead of leaving it to the missionaries.

My grandmother says people join different churches just like they buy different hats and umbrellas. My grandmother says the Catholics are just scared to death the old Priest will send them to Hell. I don't believe the one on our street would. I like him but I like his pup better. My grandmother says the Episcopalians are stuck up and some of them can strut sitting down. My grandmother says the Methodists are happy and sing loud and shout. Just plain noisy. My grandmother says the Baptists are narrow. Miss Clara Fitzpatrick is not narrow. She takes up the whole seat.

My grandmother says the Presbyterians have blue stockings, but Miss Priscilla Ross never wears hers. She reads the Bible to children on Sunday afternoons. I got so tired of Moses walking forty years and never getting to where he was going. I sure would have bought myself a mule. My grandmother says she can't tell much about the Campbellites, but I can. They say the same thing over and over. Mr. Norris always says to me, he says, "Good morning, good morning, good morning." Mrs. Bradley will tell me about the Holy Rollers tent. I am going to ask her. My mother says Mrs. Bradley has been everywhere there is to go.

Next year Bishop Jordan is going to make me an Episcopalian. I hope I don't get stuck up, but if I do I guess the Good Lord will understand. Mrs. Hare is not stuck up. She let me get in her bed when it stormed and my favorite tree blew down. I never did get to the top of that tree in peace. The butler always brought a ladder.

I hope I have not written too much. My mother says I talk too much. Judge Peters don't, I mean doesn't, think so. When he comes, he brings me a book and I play for him on the piano. I bet he sure is bored with that. The last time he came I stayed in my room eight hours, four hours for coming in to speak to him barefooted and four hours for striking the last note of my piece with my toe. After all, it was way up on the keyboard and much easier to hit with my toe than with my finger.

It is now Thursday afternoon, fifteen minutes past two o'clock and the Lord have mercy upon us all.

P.S. Mrs. Dixon, if your conscience won't let you give me an A how about a B. If that woman keeps on giving me a zero in deportment, I will simply have to see the Bishop.